Crisis on the Border:
Refugees and Undocumented Immigrants

Stuart A. Kallen

ReferencePoint
Press

San Diego, CA

© 2020 ReferencePoint Press, Inc.
Printed in the United States

For more information, contact:
ReferencePoint Press, Inc.
PO Box 27779
San Diego, CA 92198
www.ReferencePointPress.com

LIBRARY OF CONGRESS CATALOGING-IN-PUBLICATION DATA

Name: Kallen, Stuart A., 1955– author.
Title: Crisis on the Border: Refugees and Undocumented Immigrants/by Stuart A. Kallen.
Description: San Diego, CA: ReferencePoint Press, [2020] | Audience: Grade 9 to 12. | Includes
  bibliographical references and index.
Identifiers: LCCN 2019002477 (print) | LCCN 2019019975 (ebook) | ISBN 9781682827383
  (eBook) | ISBN 9781682827376 (hardback)
Subjects: LCSH: Illegal aliens—United States. | Political refugees—United States. | Illegal
  aliens—Central America. | Political refugees—Central America. | Mexican-American
  Border Region.
Classification: LCC JV6483 (ebook) | LCC JV6483 .K36 2020 (print) | DDC 325.73—dc23
LC record available at https://lccn.loc.gov/2019002477

CONTENTS

INTRODUCTION

What Sort of Crisis Is This?

For many months there has been a crisis at the US-Mexico border. But what sort of crisis is it? Americans have wildly differing views of this crisis, as evidenced by the comments of two prominent political figures. President Donald Trump has, for months, characterized events at the border as a dire threat. In a prime-time address to the nation in January 2019, Trump warned of a national security crisis: "Over the years, thousands of Americans have been brutally killed by those who illegally entered our country, and thousands more lives will be lost if we don't act right now."[1]

Critics of the president have characterized the crisis in very different terms. Nancy Pelosi, the Democratic Speaker of the House of Representatives, responded to Trump's speech this way: "The fact is: [immigrant] women and children at the border are not a security threat, they are a humanitarian challenge—a challenge that President Trump's own cruel and counterproductive policies have only deepened."[2]

The president's speech and Pelosi's response were delivered in the midst of a partial government shutdown fueled by disagreement over Trump's request for $5.7 billion to construct a new border wall. During the shutdown, thousands of federal workers endured a crisis of their own—no pay for thirty-five days. When the shutdown finally ended, the Congressional Budget Office estimated it had cost the American economy at least $11 billion.

Desperation and Hope

And then there are the many personal crises that have brought thousands of Central Americans to the southern US border in the first place. In late 2018 an estimated six thousand migrants gathered at the US-Mexico border in Tijuana (near San Diego, California). Many had traveled nearly 2,500 miles (4,000 km) across Mexico for a chance at life in the United States. This group was the second wave of migrants to arrive at the border in 2018. In April a smaller group of around fifteen hundred migrants made the same arduous journey with hopes of entering the United States.

Thousands of migrants from Central America walk north through Mexico toward the United States in October 2018. Many of the people who joined the migrant caravan told of dire conditions in their native countries.

Although the two caravans varied in size and arrived at the border at different times, the women, men, and children in both groups had much in common. The majority were from El Salvador, Guatemala, and Honduras. These three countries are menaced by government corruption, drug trafficking, and gang violence. Many people in the caravans described desperate conditions that caused them to flee, often with little more than the clothes they were wearing. Most hoped that they would be granted asylum—official protection that would allow them to legally live and work in the United States. Honduran migrant Antonio Lopez explained why he joined so many others in the caravan: "We suffered a lot in our countries and all we want is a better future."[3]

> "We suffered a lot in our countries and all we want is a better future."[3]
>
> —Honduran migrant Antonio Lopez

Trump Policies

Their timing could not have been worse. Trump had made opposition to illegal immigration the signature issue of his presidential campaign and his presidency. When Trump announced his intent to run for president in 2015, he warned that "the U.S. has become a dumping ground for everybody else's problems" and called out Mexico for sending people across the border who "have lots of problems. . . . They're bringing drugs. They're bringing crime. They're rapists. And some, I assume, are good people." To combat this problem, he vowed, "I will build a great, great wall on our southern border, and I will make Mexico pay for that wall."[4]

Trump returned to this theme again and again after he took office. When the first Central American caravan neared the border, he warned,

> The security of the United States is imperiled by a drastic surge of illegal activity on the southern border. . . . The combination of illegal drugs, dangerous gang activity, and

extensive illegal immigration not only threatens our safety but also undermines the rule of law. Our American way of life hinges on our ability . . . [to] effectively enforce our laws and protect our borders.[5]

Over the course of several months, the president took many steps aimed at preventing what he described as "an invasion of our country."[6] He ordered twenty-one hundred National Guard troops to the southern border. He ordered the arrest of anyone who entered the country illegally and authorized a plan to separate migrant parents from their children. Detention centers around the country filled to overflowing. The backlog in processing asylum claims grew from months to years. Trump once again ordered more troops to the border, this time fifty-two hundred active-duty troops. Eventually he declared a national emergency.

Many of the migrants who remained in Tijuana were traveling with small children, and their situations rapidly deteriorated. The migrants were hungry and destitute, and most were living outdoors with little shelter as winter rains swept through the city. Some Americans viewed the situation on the border as a crisis, but not the one described by the president. The crisis, as they saw it, was caused by Trump administration policies. As journalist Michael H. Fuchs writes, "There is no crisis on the border other than the humanitarian crisis of [Trump's] own making, best illustrated by the thousands of children separated from their parents."[7]

The Crises Continue

Despite ongoing political conflict in the United States, Central American men, women, and children continue to make their way toward the US border. Like the others before them, the migrants leave their homes and loved ones behind in hopes of making a new life in the United States. And as long as America represents a land of safety, stability, prosperity, and opportunity to millions of people living with violence, corruption, and poverty, the crises on the border will continue to unfold.

CHAPTER ONE

The Caravan from Central America

Edith Cruz was hoping to make her life a little easier when she opened a small tortilla-baking business with her cousin in central Honduras on October 12, 2018. But on her first day in business, Cruz was threatened by gang members. The men said they would kill her and her cousin unless they handed over half their daily profits. After the confrontation, Cruz was viewing Facebook on her cell phone when she saw a post: "An avalanche of Hondurans is preparing to leave in a caravan to the United States. Share this!"[8]

Within three hours Cruz had packed her bags and was meeting up with dozens of others gathered at the local bus station. Although Cruz learned about the caravan on Facebook, others had seen similar messages in a Whatsapp chat group named Caravana Santa Ana. The group advised travelers to pack two pairs of pants, three shirts, a sweater, water, and medicine. The caravan message went viral, spreading through Honduras, Guatemala, and El Salvador, three countries known collectively as the Northern Triangle. Within a few days large groups of people were assembling at bus terminals, town squares, and other central meeting points with plans to band together and walk north through Mexico to the US border.

> "An avalanche of Hondurans is preparing to leave in a caravan to the United States. Share this!"[8]
>
> —Facebook post

Although some took buses or managed to catch rides on passing trucks, most walked. Mothers pushed strollers with infants over potholed roads while fathers carried small children on their shoulders. According to news reports, many people in the caravan walked ten hours a day. Torrential rainstorms and temperatures above 90°F (32°C) often slowed the group's progress.

Thick bushes along the roadside served as latrines for caravan migrants. Tree-lined streams gave travelers a place to wash while seeking temporary shelter from the broiling sun. Dehydration was common and food was scarce. Many lived on a single daily meal of beans, rice, and an occasional egg. When the migrants reached villages at nightfall, they slept on sidewalks or bedded down on the floors of crowded local schoolhouses, abandoned

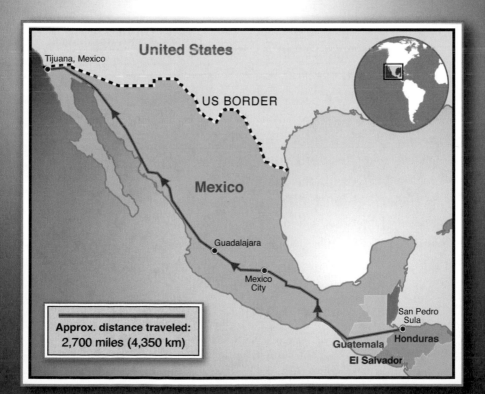

The Migrant Caravan Route, 2018

Tijuana, Mexico

United States

US BORDER

Mexico

Guadalajara

Mexico City

San Pedro Sula

Guatemala   Honduras

El Salvador

Approx. distance traveled: 2,700 miles (4,350 km)

warehouses, or churches. Maria Lourdes Aguilar, who traveled with her two daughters and four grandchildren under the age of ten, described the conditions: "On this trip you do not eat well, you do not sleep well, you never rest."[9]

Coming Together for Protection

The caravan soon swelled to more than five thousand people. Former Honduran legislator and radio show host Bartolo Fuentes said this number was roughly equal to the number of migrants who leave Honduras every month. Fuentes explained why so many were eager to join the group: "These people who have normally migrated, hidden, day after day, had decided to come together and travel together to protect themselves."[10] Fuentes was referring to the notoriously dangerous journey many migrants make through Mexico to reach the United States. Many of those who have traveled north alone or in small groups have been robbed or assaulted. They have been forced to pay bribes to corrupt officials along the way and have been overcharged by merchants for basic necessities.

In hopes of avoiding these problems, many migrants pay human smugglers called coyotes around $4,000 for safe passage, according to the Mexican Migration Project. Hiring a coyote is no guarantee of safety or even of reaching one's destination, however. Many migrants have lost all of their money to coyotes who have abandoned them along the way. Others have been injured or killed in their trek toward the border despite hiring coyotes to escort them safely to the United States.

Migrants are keenly aware of these dangers, which could explain why the caravans attracted so many people in such a short period of time. As a twenty-three-year-old mother named Carolina explained, "I was going to pay a coyote to take me

"These people who have normally migrated, hidden, day after day, had decided to come together and travel together to protect themselves."[10]

—Bartolo Fuentes, Honduran radio host

Every year tens of thousands of people flee their homes in El Salvador, Guatemala, and Honduras. These nations are ranked as some of the most violent countries in the world that are not actively engaged in war. The murder rate in this region, known as the Northern Triangle, is more than ten times higher, on average, than in the United States. Citizens in the Northern Triangle face daily violence from gangs, drug traffickers, carjackers, kidnappers, and extortionists.

Northern Triangle citizens have nowhere to turn for protection. Due to insufficient funding for law enforcement agencies, nineteen out of twenty murders remain unsolved. And citizens fear authorities as much as they do criminals. Police and soldiers are often corrupt, and some even work for drug cartels.

Women are particularity vulnerable and face a startling degree of violence from gangs, including sexual assault. According to a United Nations (UN) report, 64 percent of women in the region cited threats or attacks as their primary reason for leaving their communities. In a 2018 interview, one Salvadoran woman named Sandra described her situation: "The father of my [two] children is a gangster. He beat me a lot, and after I left him, he tried to kill us all." Sandra's husband was imprisoned for his gang activities, but other members of his gang threatened to kill her. When Sandra heard of the migrant caravan, she knew she had to take a chance and seek asylum in the United States.

Quoted in John Washington and Tracie Williams, "Portraits from the Exodus," *Nation*, December 13, 2018. www.thenation.com.

out of Honduras, but when the caravan happened it seemed so much easier."[11]

Dreams of a Better Life

Although there are no exact figures, organizations that work with the migrants say the majority were from Honduras. The others came mostly from El Salvador, Guatemala, and Nicaragua. At least twenty-three hundred were children, according to figures compiled by the United Nations Children's Fund (UNICEF). Whether they came from small villages, medium-sized towns, or big cities, most migrants shared similar harrowing stories of poverty, corruption, violence, and political repression.

Thirty-three-year-old Glenda Escobar left San Pedro Sula, Honduras—one of the most violent cities in the world—with her two youngest children, boys who were five and eight years old. Escobar had plans to attend college, but at age eighteen she was kidnapped and raped by a man she knew. Her abductor was a policeman and gang member. Escobar escaped but was pregnant. After giving birth to a daughter, Escobar married a man who fathered her two youngest sons. But he was physically abusive to her and the boys. Escobar was working as a cook and seamstress when she heard about the caravan. She quickly packed

Glenda Escobar, accompanied by two of her children, makes her way toward what she hopes will be a new life in Los Angeles. She says she fled violence and abuse in her native Honduras.

a plastic tarp, some clothes for her children, and a bar of soap. Escobar left her oldest daughter behind with relatives, promising to send for her one day. Weeks later she was walking through Mexico, headed for Los Angeles, a city where she did not know anyone. As Escobar told a reporter, "It's because in my dreams, God told me that's where he's sending me."[12]

Violent gangs such as Barrio-18 and MS-13 dominate life in much of Honduras and El Salvador. Many members of the migrant caravan were young men seeking to escape the gangs. When speaking to reporters, most did not give their full names because they feared retribution against their families back home. Sixteen-year-old Eduardo from Colón, Honduras, was one of those young men. Eduardo explained to a relief worker with the Office of the UN High Commissioner for Human Rights that MS-13 burned down his family home after he refused to join the gang: "When I saw our house burning, I knew our number had been called, our luck had run out, it was time to flee." Eduardo was able to cross into Mexico with several of his cousins who were also fleeing gangs. Eduardo expressed fears that Mexican Immigration authorities might arrest him: "I felt helpless, unwanted by any country. I thought they would send us back, and then my real nightmare would start."[13]

Like many caravan migrants, Eduardo was hoping to request asylum in the United States. According to the US Citizenship and Immigration Services (USCIS) agency, people can apply for asylum in the United States if they are "unable or unwilling to return home because they fear serious harm."[14] The federal government must consider asylum petitions whether the individuals enter the country legally or illegally. There are specific circumstances in which asylum will be granted. Poverty and unemployment are not legal reasons for granting asylum. Asylum seekers, called asylees, must show that they have a credible fear of persecution on the basis of their race, religion, nationality, political opinions, or membership in a certain social group, such as people who are lesbian, gay, bisexual, or transgender. Those who file asylum claims traditionally have remained in the United States while their cases are processed. In early 2019, federal authorities began experimenting with a new policy that would require asylum seekers to remain in Mexico while they await processing of their claims. Whether they stay in Mexico or the United States, most will have a long wait. According to the US Department of Justice, there was a backlog of approximately three hundred thousand undecided asylum cases in 2018.

Temporary Shelter in Tijuana

The first wave of Central American migrants entered the sprawling city of Tijuana—population 1.6 million—in mid-November. Once there, Mexican authorities escorted them to the Benito Juarez Sports Complex. The complex—consisting of a small stadium, basketball court, indoor gym, and Little League baseball field—is located directly across the street from the wall that marks the US-Mexico border. Within days, nearly six thousand people were living inside the facility, sleeping in thousands of tents and makeshift shelters made of plastic tarps, blankets, and sheets tied to poles and trees. As migrants continued to arrive, tents spilled out the gates of the complex onto city streets. Some slept on pieces of cardboard or on the bare ground.

The sports complex was ill equipped to deal with the thousands of migrants. The facility has two restrooms for men and two for women; each restroom has about ten toilets and six sinks. Only two of the four restrooms have small shower facilities. Long lines formed as people bathed, brushed their teeth, cleaned their children, and did laundry in the restrooms. Eighteen portable toilets were later brought into the complex, and a few dozen open-air portable showers were set up. Television crews visiting the stadium showed squalid conditions, including rotting piles of trash and open drains filled with raw sewage.

Children laughed and played in the facility despite the conditions. Reporter León Krauze described the scene:

In the small playground, kids ran up and glided down a slide. One toddler threw a toy car around while another, a girl with messy hair, pushed a tiny stroller carrying a doll. All were insufficiently dressed; many were barefoot, their legs powdered with dust.[15]

The Mexican navy set up two small kitchens that supplied free plates of beans and rice to migrants who were willing to wait for hours in long lines. The Red Cross provided medical assistance, but officials feared major epidemics as flu, pneumonia, tuberculosis, chicken pox, and other infectious diseases spread through the facility. According to Carlos Betanzos, the leader of a religious aid group, "People aren't able to take showers, they sleep on the [dirt], nobody is cleaning the bathrooms, so conditions are there for a major infection."[16] Conditions at the sports complex further deteriorated after a torrential rainstorm hit Tijuana in November. People were forced to wade through deep puddles and sleep in the mud.

Hundreds of migrants wait in line for food in November 2018 after having reached Tijuana, a Mexican city on the US-Mexico border. Despite efforts by the Mexican government and various humanitarian organizations, living conditions for migrants proved challenging.

Caravan migrants traveling over Mexican roads on the long journey to the US border in late 2018 faced immeasurable hardships. Most people had little or no money. Many walked hundreds of miles in flip-flops, torn sneakers, and rubber clogs. Traveling thousands of miles on foot is difficult for anyone, but the journey was particularly hard for those with disabilities. Despite the difficulties, hundreds of migrants made the journey using crutches and wheelchairs.

Honduran Rafael Peralta has a clubfoot, a deformed foot that is twisted so that the sole cannot be placed flat on the ground. Peralta walked thousands of miles from Honduras to the migrant camp in the Benito Juarez Sports Complex in Tijuana using crutches and a wheelchair given to him by the Red Cross. But maneuvering through the muddy sports complex on crutches was difficult. He could not carry plates of food handed out by volunteers. And it was nearly impossible for him to use the showers or crowded, filthy bathrooms in the sports complex. According to Peralta, "It is very difficult to bathe in this place; sometimes I spend four or five days without bathing. . . . If I try to enter the latrine with the crutches I can slip." Peralta and others with disabilities could use private bathrooms and showers nearby, but these facilities charged around $1.25 for each use. Peralta sold cigarettes in camp to make extra money so he could bathe once or twice a week.

Quoted in Carlos Ríos Espinosa, "Life with a Disability in the Migrant Camp," Human Rights Watch, December 20, 2018. www.hrw.org.

Frustration Grows

Although the migrants had reached the border, most had no real idea of how to proceed with their requests for asylum. Before they left their homes, few probably had any idea where they were going (other than to the United States) and what they would do once they got there. As journalist Jonathan Blitzer wrote, "Many of them haven't thought that far in advance. . . . The travelers are basically improvising."[17]

Those who expected to quickly cross the border and officially request asylum learned early on that this would not be possible.

First, the Trump administration tried to block the migrants from entering the United States to make their claims. When a federal judge ruled against this move, US authorities announced that they would process only about thirty to sixty asylum claims each day. At that rate, migrants could expect a wait of at least four months just to submit an asylum request, the first step in a long process.

As living conditions deteriorated in the sports complex and the number of asylum seekers continued to grow, many migrants grew desperate. Some abandoned any hope of an orderly entry. As darkness fell each night, groups of migrants gathered at the border fence that separates Tijuana and San Diego and runs all the way to the Pacific Ocean. Even at this heavily patrolled stretch of border, migrants could squeeze through breaks in the fence or climb over pylons. And many, including mothers carrying young children, were able to do so. Once across the border, most surrendered to Border Patrol agents waiting on the US side.

On November 25, 2018, the frustration with the slow pace of the asylum claims process exploded into chaos. A scheduled Sunday morning protest at the San Ysidro port of entry on the Mexican side of the border attracted several hundred migrants. Suddenly, dozens of protesters decided to rush the border. Some tried to climb fences, and others attempted to run through the car lanes leading into the United States. Thirty-seven-year-old Honduran Elizabeth Chirinos said she ran toward the border because she felt desperate: "The U.S. isn't letting us through, and I can't live in those conditions in the [stadium]. I want to go to the U.S. and not stay in Mexico, because there are more opportunities."[18]

"I want to go to the U.S. and not stay in Mexico, because there are more opportunities."[18]

—Elizabeth Chirinos, Honduran migrant

Some protesters threw rocks and bottles at Border Patrol agents stationed on the US side of the border. The agents responded by firing tear gas at the protesters—none of whom managed to breach the border. Panic ensued. Protesters and bystanders alike choked on clouds of tear gas. More than forty protesters, mostly young men, were arrested.

After the protesters were dispersed, the Border Patrol closed all vehicle and foot traffic through the San Ysidro port of entry. About 175,000 people typically cross the border (in a legal and orderly fashion) at this location on a typical Sunday. The border was reopened later that night. The vast majority of waiting migrants took no part in this incident; they only learned of it by word of mouth. It was big news in the United States, however. Hours later Trump tweeted, "Mexico should move the flag waving Migrants . . . back to their countries. Do it by plane, do it by bus, do it anyway you want, but they are NOT coming into the U.S.A. We will close the Border permanently if need be."[19]

"Mexico should move the flag waving Migrants . . . back to their countries. . . . They are NOT coming into the U.S.A. We will close the Border permanently."[19]

—Donald Trump, president of the United States

Americans Have Mixed Views

Americans watched all of these events unfold with mixed feelings. A poll by the Monmouth University Polling Institute, conducted in November 2018 at the height of the caravan controversy, found that many Americans considered the migrant caravan to represent some sort of threat to the nation. Polling results showed that 29 percent saw the caravan as a major threat and 24 percent saw it as a minor threat. Another 39 percent said they did not believe the caravan represented any threat to the nation. In that same poll, however, 70 percent of Americans said the migrants should be allowed to enter the United States if they meet certain requirements, such as being able to show they were persecuted in their home countries. This was in contrast to 26 percent who said they should be immediately returned to their home countries once they reached the border.

Claims made by the president and members of his administration about the character of the migrants also generated a mixed response. Trump and others have said that there were foreign terrorists among the migrants. Half of those surveyed in the Monmouth poll said they either did not believe (22 percent) or thought it unlikely (28 percent) that there were foreign terrorists among the migrants. However, 25 percent of survey respondents said they believed the president's claim to be true, and 13 percent said they were unsure but leaned toward believing this claim.

People in different regions of the country have also been shown to have a variety of opinions about the events occurring at the US-Mexico border. According to the same Monmouth poll, people in border states, who would be most affected by the caravans, were less worried about them than people in other parts of the country. Only 21 percent of border-state residents (those in California, Arizona, New Mexico, and Texas) saw the caravans as a major threat. This differed from most other regions of the country. The caravans were seen as a major threat by 35 percent of residents in the Southeast; 33 percent in the Midwest; 33 percent in the Rocky Mountain–Northwest region; and 25 percent in the Northeast.

An Uncertain Future

By early 2019, most migrants had come to realize that the process for requesting asylum could take many months or, in some cases, not happen at all. Hundreds had voluntarily returned home. Thousands applied for visas to live and work in Mexico for a one-year period. An unknown number had crossed the border illegally. Still others waited in various Mexican border towns, where they planned to wait their turn to make their case for asylum. As Honduran Douglas Mautute explained, "A lot of people are leaving because there is no solution here [in Tijuana]. We thought they would let us in. But Trump sent the military instead of social workers."[20]

Driven by poverty, hunger, and fear, most migrants do not believe things will get better at home. Until conditions improve in the Northern Triangle, thousands of people will continue to make the dangerous journey north, eating and sleeping where they can while hoping that a better future awaits them.

CHAPTER TWO

Refugees in Search of a Safe Haven

On December 10, 2018, media outlets throughout the world noted a special anniversary. It had been seventy years since the United States led the efforts to create the Universal Declaration of Human Rights (UDHR). The thirty articles of the declaration were approved by the UN General Assembly in 1948 and have since been translated into five hundred languages. According to historian Jennifer Vannette, the UDHR "created a common language of human rights where none had existed before."[21] The declaration states that human rights are universal, transcend borders, and form "the foundation of freedom, justice and peace in the world." The UDHR specifically addresses the issue of refugees fleeing hostile nations: "Everyone has the right to seek and to enjoy in other countries asylum from persecution."[22]

> "Everyone has the right to seek and to enjoy in other countries asylum from persecution."[22]
>
> —The Universal Declaration of Human Rights, passed by the United Nations in 1948

The United States led the efforts to create the UDHR. And America's emphasis on human rights has long provided a beacon of hope to oppressed people throughout the world. Since 1948, millions have traveled to the United States from Poland, Cuba, Iran, and dozens of other nations to seek asylum and find freedom, justice, and peace. However, the number of migrants seeking asylum in the United States has rapidly multiplied. In 2008, according to the US Department of Homeland Security (DHS), only one in one hundred border crossers sought asylum. In 2018 that number grew to one in three, or around 130,000 people. And in 2019 asylum seekers continued to arrive at the southern US border.

Processing Asylum Claims

Asylum is a legal status that governments grant to people who have sought safety from persecution or risk of persecution in their home countries. Under US and international law, any foreign-born person has a legal right to ask for asylum in another country. To do so in the United States, asylum seekers can surrender themselves to officers at any field office operated by Customs and

A US Border Patrol agent speaks with a young woman from El Salvador who illegally crossed into the United States. Foreign-born individuals have a legal right to ask for asylum in the United States, whether they enter the country legally or illegally.

Border Protection (CBP). They can approach a Border Patrol officer at any airport or other port of entry. They can request asylum whether they enter the country legally or illegally.

Whichever way they enter the country, asylum seekers go through an initial screening interview (although that interview might not take place for several weeks or months). That first screening is with an officer who works for USCIS. The asylum officer conducts a short question-and-answer session called a credible fear interview. During this interview, migrants testify under oath as to the reason for their asylum petition. To be granted a full hearing, migrants must show that they have a genuine fear of persecution in their home countries. They must convince the asylum officer that they risk beating, torture, arrest, or murder if they return to their home countries.

After hearing a claimant's case, the officer decides whether that migrant's fear of persecution is credible. In June 2018, according to analysis by Syracuse University's Transactional Records Access Clearinghouse (TRAC), only 15 percent of these initial interviews resulted in a finding of credible fear. This is less than the prior year, when close to 30 percent of asylum seekers were found to have a credible fear of persecution. This finding does not guarantee that an individual will be granted asylum; rather, it allows the person to move to the next step in the process: a hearing before an immigration judge.

Those who do not pass the first interview are generally deported within a few weeks. Most of those who do pass are released from custody and ordered to appear later before an immigration judge. It can be years before that hearing takes place. The immigration courts have only 330 judges around the country. In August 2018 the average wait for an immigration hearing was 721 days, according to the immigrant advocate organization National Immigration Forum.

Migrants waiting for their day in court are free to stay in the United States under certain conditions. Some are required to post a bond, money that is returned when the immigrant shows

Immigration judges who handle asylum cases are often required to make heart-rending decisions. In a 2016 editorial, immigration judge Thomas G. Snow described the difficulties he faces every day:

> Someone facing physical abuse (or worse) back home, depending on the reasons for such persecution, may be eligible for asylum and can stay. A person with U.S. citizen children . . . and whose kids would suffer "exceptional and extremely unusual hardship" if the parent is deported—can stay.
>
> Deciding such cases doesn't sound so difficult. But it often is. . . . One of our most vexing challenges is assessing credibility—trying to figure out whether the person is telling the truth about what he fears and why. Sometimes, there is not much to go on other than the person's own testimony. Yet this is not a decision we want to get wrong. I've probably been fooled and granted asylum to some who didn't deserve it. I hope and pray I have not denied asylum to some who did. . . .
>
> So we sometimes have to order fine people . . . deported to places they barely remember—in decisions often delivered orally, in court, in front of sobbing kids and desperate spouses. . . . Because we are judges, we do our best to follow the law and apply it impartially to the people who appear before us. I know I do so, even when it breaks my heart.

Thomas G. Snow, "The Gut-Wrenching Life of an Immigration Judge," *USA Today*, December 12, 2016. www.usatoday.com.

up for a court hearing. Others are obligated to check in regularly with immigration officials. According to the *New York Times*, in 2018 around eighty thousand migrants were compelled to wear ankle monitors—tamper-resistant, electronic devices fastened to the ankle. These devices are programmed to allow wearers the freedom to travel within a specified area. Ankle monitors send an alarm to authorities if the wearer travels outside the permitted area or if the device is damaged or removed.

The bond and the monitoring system ensure that 95 percent of asylum seekers show up for their court hearings. And although asylum proceedings look like criminal trials, immigration courts operate differently than courts that consider criminal matters. In criminal cases, the burden of proof is on the government. This means a person is considered innocent until a government prosecutor proves that the person is guilty of committing a crime. In immigration court, the burden of proof is on the asylum seekers. They have to show why they should be granted asylum.

And they often must do so without the aid of a lawyer. Asylum seekers do not have the constitutional protections afforded those accused of crimes. Unlike criminal defendants, they do not have the right to a court-appointed lawyer. This means migrants must either hire a lawyer at their own expense or navigate the complex immigration system alone. All hearings are conducted in English, a language many migrants do not speak. And some who seek asylum are children or teens. In 2018 over twenty-six hundred children, including more than one hundred under age five, appeared before immigration judges to ask for asylum.

Outcomes Vary Widely

Faced with numerous hurdles, most migrants fail in their quest for asylum in the United States. According to Syracuse University's TRAC, around 22 percent of asylum seekers from Guatemala, Honduras, and El Salvador were granted asylum in 2018. TRAC reports that denial rates varied depending on the specific judge assigned to a case. The example of two women from the Honduran capital, Tegucigalpa, illustrates this point.

Sandra and Ana, who did not want their full names to be used, both told nearly identical stories in immigration court. In 2013 the women were on the board of a parent-teacher association at their children's school. The group planned to help local mothers work together in an effort to drive out vicious gang members who tormented students on campus. Both women were targeted by gangs that vowed to kill them and their children. Separately, the women made the dangerous journey across Mexico with their children and turned themselves in to the Border Patrol. Both requested asylum for themselves and their children.

Both women passed the initial credible fear screening. Sandra was released and allowed to join her husband, who was living in San Francisco. Ana was also released. She moved in with her daughter in Charlotte, North Carolina. Sandra's asylum case was heard by Judge Dalin Holyoak in San Francisco in 2016. The judge granted her asylum request. In North Carolina, Ana's case was heard by Judge Stuart Crouch in 2016. He denied the asylum request and ordered Ana to report for deportation. According to an analysis by the Reuters news agency, Crouch rejected about 89 percent of asylum petitions that came before him. Holyoak, on the other hand, denied asylum in 43 percent of the cases he heard.

The Reuters study found similar variations in immigration courts across the country. In New York, one judge granted asylum 93 percent of the time, but a judge in Houston only did so 4 percent of the time. Karen Musalo, the director of the Center for Gender & Refugee Studies at the University of California Hastings College of Law in San Francisco, states, "It is clearly troubling when you have these kinds of gross disparities. These are life or death matters. . . . Whether you win or whether you lose shouldn't depend on the roll of the dice of which judge gets your case."[23]

Ana was able to appeal her case—and she was allowed to remain in the country during that process. Most of those who lose their asylum cases cannot afford to continue with the appeals process and are sent back to their countries of origin. This can be a death sentence for some. According to a 2016 study by Columbia University's Global Migration Project, at least sixty migrants were killed or seriously wounded after they were sent back to their home countries. Immigrant advocates say the number is far higher; the government does not keep track of what happens to asylum seekers who are deported, so there is no way of knowing the exact toll.

Zero Tolerance

The US asylum process, which had been in place for decades, was changed in April 2018. That month the Trump administration enacted a new zero-tolerance policy. Under this policy, every adult caught entering the United States illegally—regardless of whether he or she was seeking asylum—was to be arrested, detained, and charged with improper entry. This is considered a minor offense, a federal misdemeanor punishable by fines and up to six months in prison. Repeat offenders charged with the more serious offense of illegal reentry could be jailed for two years.

Once the zero-tolerance policy was enacted, the Border Patrol began arresting everyone entering the country illegally, including parents traveling with children. Until 2015, families with children crossing the border illegally were often detained

Migrants await processing at a detention facility in Texas in 2018. Under the Trump administration's zero-tolerance policy, parents were separated from children to deter Central American families from seeking asylum.

together in family detention centers. However, a federal judge ruled that families could not be held for more than twenty days, and children could not be detained in federal jails. After the ruling, President Barack Obama's administration released families rather than separate them. But under the Trump administration's zero-tolerance policy, children were separated from their parents. The children were turned over to a federal agency called the Office of Refugee Resettlement (ORR) that is overseen by the US Department of Health and Human Services (HHS). The children, some as young as eighteen months old, were categorized by the ORR as unaccompanied minors. This designation was previously only used for minors who crossed the border on their own.

The policy of separating children from their parents was enacted to discourage, or deter, potential asylum seekers from traveling to the United States. As HHS assistant secretary Steven Wagner explained to reporters in a 2018 conference call, "We expect that the new policy will result in a deterrence effect, we certainly hope that parents stop bringing their kids on this dangerous journey and entering the country illegally."[24]

Migrant Youth Shelters

During a six-week period following the enactment of the zero-tolerance policy, around two thousand children were separated from the adults with whom they had crossed the border. Around one thousand of the children taken from their parents were under age ten, according to data obtained by the *New York Times*.

The children were detained while authorities searched for American relatives or sponsors who would care for the kids while their parents' immigration cases were pending. However, this was a slow, difficult process made worse by the administration's demands that sponsors submit fingerprints and other data that would be shared with immigration authorities. Since many potential sponsors themselves were undocumented, few were willing to step forward to shelter the children.

The growing number of young detainees overwhelmed the HHS system of migrant youth shelters that were originally set up to hold a much smaller number of unaccompanied minors who crossed the border. Most children were put in the care of private contractors who operate one hundred shelters in seventeen states. Some of the shelters were set up in warehouses, offices, and abandoned big-box stores. In September 2018 the Trump administration increased shelter capacity by tripling the size of a massive tent city in Tornillo, Texas, which eventually held thirty-eight hundred children. *New York Times* reporters describe the shelters as "a rough blend of boarding school, day care center and medium security lockup."[25]

> "[Youth detention facilities are] a rough blend of boarding school, day care center and medium security lockup."[25]
>
> —*New York Times* reporters

Babies and toddlers under the age of four were held in what the government classifies as tender-age shelters. These facilities are legally required to meet state licensing standards for child welfare agencies. Inspectors who visited three tender-age shelters located in the Rio Grande Valley in South Texas said the facilities were clean and safe. However, doctors and psychologists say that separating young children from parents can cause long-term psychological damage.

Facilities that confined older children and teens varied from place to place. Shelters that were constructed inside warehouses held children in areas surrounded by chain-link fencing. The Spanish-speaking youths referred to the cold concrete cell as *la hielera*—"the freezer"—and the fenced cages as *la perrera*—"the dog kennel." Detainees were given thin sleeping pads and silver Mylar blankets like those used in disaster areas. Not all shelters were as bad as the so-called kennels, though. A youth shelter with a pool and sports fields in Yonkers, north of New York City, was compared to a summer camp.

In November 2018 Wilder Hilario Maldonado Cabrera walked into an immigration courtroom in San Antonio, Texas. Wilder was born in a rural mountain village in El Salvador and had entered the United States illegally with his father, Hilario, the previous June. He was in court without a lawyer to ask Judge Anibal Martinez for asylum. The judge asked the defendant his age, and Wilder replied in Spanish that he was six years old. While he was the youngest defendant in court that day, he was not the only minor. A few times a month the waiting rooms in America's immigration courts resemble day care centers. They are filled with toys, coloring books, and stuffed animals. On these days, children as young as four years old stand alone before immigration judges.

Wilder, who was in temporary foster care, did not know his father was being held in federal custody in Texas and was facing deportation. Hilario's request for asylum was turned down because of a minor crime he had committed while living as an undocumented immigrant in the United States more than a decade earlier. Although the crime would never result in loss of custody in criminal court, immigration authorities use minor nonviolent criminal records to separate children from parents. Hilario appealed the decision. The judge decided to set aside any decisions on Wilder's case until he could be represented by a volunteer lawyer. Until that time, the young boy and hundreds like him face an uncertain future in the US immigration system.

Reaction

By June 2018 the Trump administration's family separation policy was creating a steady stream of media reports that produced widespread outrage. Even some of Trump's strongest Republican supporters, including Representative Paul Ryan and Senator Orrin Hatch, objected to the policy. As Barbara Bush, First Lady from 1989 to 1993, wrote shortly before her death in 2018, "This zero-tolerance policy is cruel. It is immoral. And it breaks my heart. Our government should not be in the business of warehousing

Flanked by DHS secretary Kirstjen Nielsen and Vice President Mike Pence, in June 2018 President Donald Trump signs an executive order ending family separation at the border.

children in converted box stores or making plans to place them in tent cities in the desert outside of El Paso."[26]

On June 18 secretary of DHS Kirstjen Nielsen held a press conference to defend the policy. Nielsen said the children were being well cared for and were able to communicate with their parents through phone calls and videoconferencing. Nielsen also defended the family separation policy: "Parents who entered illegally are, by definition, criminals. . . . By entering our country illegally, often in dangerous circumstances, illegal immigrants put their children at risk."[27]

Nielsen's press conference did little to alleviate public and political opposition to the policy. On

"Our government should not be in the business of warehousing children in converted box stores or making plans to place them in tent cities in the desert outside of El Paso."[26]

—Former First Lady Barbara Bush

June 20, Trump signed an executive order ending family separation at the border. The administration offered a new plan that would keep families together in detention while asylum claims were pending.

Desperate to Reunite

When Trump signed the executive order to end family separation, he did not address the issue of those who were already separated. But on June 26, 2018, a federal judge in California ordered the administration to reunite all children with their parents within fourteen days. However, the family separation policy was carried out in a chaotic and disorganized manner that made reuniting families difficult.

When the ORR initially separated children from families, all individuals were given identification bracelets and computer registration numbers to keep children and parents connected. But after migrants were processed by the ORR, they were turned over to CBP. This agency is tasked with holding illegal border crossers for the first seventy-two hours after they enter the country. In hundreds of cases, CBP deleted or ignored the records created by the ORR and gave the migrants different identification numbers. This was done in the belief that it made more sense for CBP to track individuals separately rather than as part of a family unit. The problems created by the bureaucratic missteps were made worse by revelations that some parents were deported while their children remained in shelters in the United States.

By early September some of the reunification efforts were successful, but problems continued. Around 500 minors, including 22 children younger than five, were still in custody. Around 125 of these children who lived with American relatives were granted parental permission to remain in the United States. This was difficult for parents who missed their kids but wanted them to have a better life in America.

A Father and Son Separated

A study by the independent news organization ProPublica described one 2018 case. The report says CBP pulled a four-year-old Salvadoran boy named Brayan out of the arms of his father, Julio, who had crossed the border in Texas. (The father was identified by his first name only because he was fleeing gang violence and worried about relatives back home.) Julio was taken into custody after asking for asylum, and Brayan was sent to a foster care agency in New York City. The agency had no knowledge that Brayan had been separated from his father by CBP.

When ProPublica contacted border officials, those officials described Julio as a member of the notorious MS-13 gang. Julio contended this was not the case. Julio hired lawyer Georgia Evangelista to help him regain custody of his son. According to Evangelista, when Julio arrived at the border in September, he carried a letter from a Salvadoran lawyer that described his reasons for seeking asylum. Julio had been attacked and threatened by gang members for years. His former employer vouched for his character and said he never engaged in criminal activity.

When Evangelista tried to find out more about the case, CBP refused to answer any questions. Agents claimed Julio's alleged activities were confidential due to an ongoing investigation. According to Evangelista, "I don't know what information, if any, they really have on Julio. They have total discretion when it comes to separating him from his child. They can do what they want. And they don't have to explain why."[28] As the case worked its way through various courts and government agencies, Brayan remained in foster care, too young to understand where his father had gone.

Without any explanation, in December 2018 the government reversed course and reunited Brayan with his father after eleven weeks of separation. The homecoming was a happy one, but Julio's asylum case remained unresolved as he awaited his day in immigration court. Brayan and Julio put a human face on an asylum system that once offered hope to desperate people from around the world but has undergone many changes that have greatly narrowed those hopes. "President Trump has said that migrants are exploiting the asylum system by making baseless and fraudulent claims in order to remain in the United States," writes *New York Times* reporter Miriam Jordan.

> His administration has taken a number of steps to make the process harder, including narrowing the grounds for winning asylum, limiting the number of asylum seekers who can be processed at the border each day and requiring some applicants to wait in Mexico while their cases make their way through the courts.[29]

These and other changes mean that people fleeing persecution and violence may not receive the freedom, justice, and peace enshrined in the words of the UDHR.

CHAPTER THREE

The Undocumented Immigrants

In 2018 the US president warned that America was being "overrun by masses of illegal aliens."[30] Although federal government statistics show a steady downward trend in illegal immigration since 2000, that changed in 2018 and has continued into 2019. The most common measure of illegal immigration is the number of undocumented immigrants arrested along the US-Mexico border. This number is considered a reasonable way to measure illegal immigration using the idea that fewer arrests mean fewer illegal crossings. According to the DHS, in 2017 the Border Patrol "recorded the lowest level of illegal cross-border migration on record, as measured by apprehensions along the border and inadmissible encounters at U.S. ports of entry."[31] The report shows an 80 percent drop in arrests, from about 1.6 million in 2000 to approximately 300,000 in 2017.

In 2018, however, arrest rates soared as asylum-seeking families fleeing violence and poverty in Central America crossed the border illegally. In February 2019 alone, the government reported, border agents arrested seventy-six thousand people (mostly families or unaccompanied minors) along the southern border. This is double the number of arrests from the same time the previous year.

Who Are the Undocumented Immigrants?

Regardless of fluctuations in illegal crossings, approximately 11 million undocumented immigrants already live in the United States. It is difficult to establish the exact size, economic status, and location of this group; undocumented immigrants rarely participate in research because they fear it might lead to deportation. However, in 2014 the DHS conducted one of the few studies about illegal immigration available. It compiled statistics using government figures and research conducted by the Pew Research Center and the Center for Immigration Studies. The DHS study revealed that more than 75 percent of undocumented immigrants had lived in the United States for more than ten years. Around half of the undocumented immigrants were from Mexico, 15 percent were from Central America, 12 percent were from Asia, and most of the rest were from South America, the Caribbean, Europe, and Canada. Around 60 percent of undocumented immigrants lived in California, Texas, Florida, New York, New Jersey, and Illinois.

Studies by the DHS and other groups have added some additional information on who makes up the undocumented immigrant population. For instance, 10 percent of undocumented immigrants—more than 1 million people—owned a business at the time of the DHS study. And, according to an analysis of census data by the Migration Policy Institute, more than 3.4 million undocumented immigrants, or 31 percent, owned their own homes.

The DHS study also showed that the era of mass entry by undocumented immigrants seeking work in the United States was over. The population of undocumented workers in the United States reached a high of 12.2 million in 2008, but that number has moved downward ever since. Researchers say the shrinking number reflects economic realities. More than 1 million people went back to their native countries after the 2008 recession wiped out millions of jobs that attracted undocumented immigrants.

Ruben Moroyoqui (second from left and surrounded by family) was fighting deportation in 2018. The Arizona mechanic legally entered the United States about sixteen years earlier but overstayed his visa.

Although many of those undocumented immigrants entered the United States illegally, a significant number did not. A large segment of the undocumented immigrant population consists of foreigners who obtain a visa to enter the country legally but stay after the visa expires. The DHS estimates that every year around half a million people enter the country legally with three- to six-month visas but violate the law by remaining in the United States after the documents expire. Exact figures are not available, but various estimates claim that visa overstays make up a third to more than half of all undocumented immigrants in the country. According to a 2017 DHS report, Canadians account for the largest group of visa overstays—ninety-two thousand in 2017. Mexicans make up the second-largest group, with around half that number.

Granting Amnesty

Visa overstays and illegal crossings have been occurring for decades; these events are not new. Concerns about undocumented immigrants are also not new. In 1972, for instance, a headline in the

U.S. News & World Report proclaimed, "Surge of Illegal Immigrants Across American Borders: Never Before Have So Many Aliens Swarmed Illegally into U.S.—Millions Moving Across Nation."[32] That article, and others published around that time, featured photos of young men wading across the Rio Grande on the Texas-Mexico border or crowds of immigrants crashing through border stations in California and Arizona on foot. The tone set by the articles was often one of panic. Illegal immigration was described as an alien invasion, an uncontrolled hemorrhage of people, and a costly nightmare.

Although there are no exact figures, the government estimated that during the 1970s and 1980s between 500,000 and 1.5 million people entered the United States illegally every year. About 80 percent of these people were from Mexico, but there were also people from Central America, the Caribbean, and elsewhere. A Roper Center poll from that time showed that 91 percent of Americans supported an all-out effort to stop illegal immigration. However, powerful agricultural interests wanted the cheap supply of labor provided by undocumented immigrants who worked in fruit and vegetable fields.

Congress addressed the conflicts over illegal immigration in 1986, when it passed a sweeping bipartisan bill that granted amnesty to undocumented immigrants who had lived continuously in the United States between 1982 and 1986. The Immigration Reform and Control Act was signed by Republican president Ronald Reagan. Reagan believed that the United States should be open to anyone who wanted to work hard and improve the country. As Reagan commented in 1984, "I believe in the idea of amnesty for those who have put down roots and lived here, even though some time back they may have entered [the country] illegally."[33]

> "I believe in the idea of amnesty for those who have put down roots and lived here, even though some time back they may have entered [the country] illegally."[33]
>
> —Ronald Reagan, the fortieth president of the United States

This immigration reform act gave legal status to about 2.7 million people who were living in the United States illegally at the time. It was the largest immigrant legalization program in US history. However, this amnesty did not stop illegal immigration. Employers continued to demand cheap labor. Drawn by economic opportunities, millions of people continued to enter the United States illegally, and the number of undocumented immigrants kept climbing.

The Underground Economy

The jobs being filled by undocumented workers then are essentially the same jobs they fill today. According to a 2018 study by Cornell University, more than half of all farmworkers in the United States are undocumented immigrants. These workers play an im-

Migrant farmworkers pick strawberries in central California. A 2018 Cornell University study found that more than half of all farmworkers in the United States were undocumented immigrants.

portant role in the agriculture industry. If federal policies reduced the number of undocumented workers by 50 percent, the Cornell study notes, more than thirty-five hundred dairy farms would go out of business, causing milk prices to double. The fruit, vegetable, and meat industries would face similar problems; production would drop and prices would spike.

Undocumented workers fill many other roles, according to the Cornell study. They make up 25 percent of all maids and house and office cleaners and around 15 percent of construction workers. No matter which jobs they do, the wages for undocumented immigrants are almost always less than the wages for legal US workers. And few undocumented workers receive benefits such as overtime pay or health insurance. However, undocumented workers usually receive higher pay for jobs they do in the United States than they would for similar jobs in their home countries.

> "Our government (under both parties) has always been aware that US companies recruit workers in the poorest parts of Mexico for cheap labor."[34]
>
> —College professor Michelle Martin

In this sense, undocumented workers benefit from being in the US labor market. The overall US economy benefits as well. Cornell University professor Michelle Martin, who was part of the team that conducted the 2018 study, describes an underground economy in which the labor of low-paid workers adds to the broader US economy:

> We are a country that has an above-ground system of immigration and an underground system. Our government (under both parties) has always been aware that US companies recruit workers in the poorest parts of Mexico for cheap labor, and . . . [the immigration service] has looked the other way because this underground economy benefits our country to the tune of billions of dollars annually.[34]

The Deportation Force

US presidents have differed in their responses to this underground economy and to concerns about illegal immigration in general. As it turns out, political party is not necessarily an indicator of that response. Reagan, a Republican, signed off on the largest amnesty bill in US history. Under President George W. Bush, also a Republican, there was an increase in the number of workplace raids at businesses suspected of hiring undocumented workers. President Barack Obama, a Democrat, cut back on the number of workplace raids but ordered businesses to provide documentation that their employees were in the country legally.

Obama also tripled the budget for immigration enforcement. However, he directed Immigration and Customs Enforcement (ICE) to focus on undocumented immigrants who had committed violent crimes or were repeat offenders, as well as anyone who had recently crossed the border. During Obama's eight years in office, these policies resulted in the deportation of 3 million undocumented immigrants. This record prompted critics in the immigration rights community to label Obama the "deporter in chief."[35]

President Trump, a Republican, expanded immigration enforcement efforts as soon as he took office in 2017. During the first week of his administration, Trump signed a series of executive orders to drastically increase the number of deportations. One order directed ICE to hire ten thousand new officers to round up undocumented immigrants already living in the United States. Another executive order increased the number of workplace raids around the country.

One of Trump's goals was to deport people as quickly as possible. To make this happen, he changed what is called the expedited removals process. Expedited removals, sometimes called fast-track deportation, concern undocumented immigrants who have been in the country for a short time period. Those who fall into this category do not have the right to see an immigration judge. They can be deported immediately. Obama had used this tool as well, but he applied it to individuals who had been in the country for two weeks or less. Trump expanded the time period

More than fifteen hundred undocumented workers were arrested in workplace raids during 2018. One such raid took place at a slaughterhouse in Morristown, Tennessee. On April 5, 2018, one hundred ICE agents arrived in a fleet of sport-utility vehicles as a helicopter circled overhead to provide air support. The agents, dressed in military-style camouflage, entered the plant with guns drawn. Workers were ordered to put their hands in the air as they were lined up, searched, and restrained with handcuffs. ICE arrested 129 individuals. Some had legal status and were let go after several hours in detention. Thirty-two of those arrested, mostly people with health issues and parents of young children, were also released. Seventeen were immediately deported. About forty workers were released on bond while their cases wound through immigration courts.

In February 2019, nearly a year after the raid, five remained in detention in out-of-state facilities. After the raid, about one hundred children in Morristown were left without one or both of their parents. Because of the huge backlog of cases in immigration courts, most will have to wait several years before their cases are resolved. Some will eventually be deported.

According to the DHS, the owner of the slaughterhouse was charged with tax evasion, labor violations, and employing undocumented workers. He faced the possibility of twenty-five years in prison. However, he was free on bond—and his slaughterhouse continued to operate—while his lawyers fought the charges against him.

for expedited removals to include people who had arrived in the United States during the previous two years.

Trump also did away with the emphasis on deporting violent criminals and repeat offenders. He expanded the pool of people prioritized for deportation. The expanded pool includes people who have been charged with crimes but have not been convicted. It also includes people who have committed misdemeanor crimes. These are generally low-level, nonviolent crimes such as marijuana possession or shoplifting. In the world of immigration law, these are called chargeable criminal offenses.

Deported

There are other chargeable criminal offenses that can lead to deportation. The act of obtaining false documents, such as birth certificates, driver's licenses, and Social Security cards, is one such offense. Anyone who has lived and worked illegally for any period of time in the United States has probably obtained such documents, putting them on a fast track to deportation if they are caught.

This is what happened to Samuel Oliver-Bruno in 2018. Oliver-Bruno, a native of Mexico, had lived off and on in Durham, North Carolina, since 1994. His wife and son are American citizens. He is not. He was working in the construction industry when his father got sick in 2011. Oliver-Bruno went back to Mexico to care for his father. Then, in 2014, while Oliver-Bruno was still in Mexico, his wife developed a life-threatening disease that required open-heart surgery. He was anxious to return to the United States to care for her.

In hopes of assuring his ability to reenter the United States, Oliver-Bruno bought a counterfeit birth certificate in Mexico. He presented the birth certificate to a US border agent, who immediately recognized it as a forgery. Oliver-Bruno was arrested and charged with using false or misleading information to enter the country illegally. When he appeared in immigration court, Oliver-Bruno showed the judge his wife's medical records. In line with policies in force in 2014, the judge issued a stay of removal. The stay allowed Oliver-Bruno to remain in the United States as long as he reapplied every year.

Oliver-Bruno did this each year, and each year he received another stay—until 2017. That year, when he entered the USCIS office in Charlotte to extend his stay of removal, he was told he would be deported because he had committed a chargeable criminal offense.

Upon receiving the news, Oliver-Bruno sought refuge in the CityWell United Methodist Church in nearby Durham. CityWell is a part of the faith-based sanctuary movement. It consists of about eleven hundred churches nationwide that offer undocumented immigrants a place to live while they pursue their legal cases. ICE agents traditionally have not arrested immigrants in locations such as churches, schools, and health care facilities. However, after Trump became president, ICE agents began arresting people coming and going from such facilities. Undocumented immigrants have been detained while dropping off their children at school or exiting hospitals and churches. In one August 2018 case, a man in San Bernardino, California, was arrested by ICE as he was taking his pregnant wife to a hospital as she was about to give birth.

ICE sometimes coordinates with other immigration agencies to lure undocumented immigrants out of sanctuaries. This is what happened to Oliver-Bruno. After living in the basement of City-Well for more than a year, in 2018 he was told that USCIS would consider extending his stay of removal, but he needed to come to the office to submit his paperwork. If he did not keep the appointment, he was told, an order for deportation would be issued immediately. Oliver-Bruno knew it was a risk, but he went anyway. When Oliver-Bruno entered the USCIS office, he was immediately arrested and taken to an ICE holding facility in Georgia. Within a week, he was deported to Mexico.

The Dreamers

One group of undocumented immigrants received a temporary reprieve from deportation in 2012. This is the group of young people known as Dreamers. They get their name from the Development, Relief, and Education for Alien Minors (DREAM) Act, a proposed law designed to grant permanent legal residency to children who were brought into the country illegally by their parents. The DREAM Act was introduced in Congress three times — in 2001, 2007, and 2011 — and failed to pass each time. In response, Obama issued an executive order creating the Deferred Action for Childhood Arrivals (DACA) program. This program did not provide official legal status or a pathway to citizenship, but it allowed dreamers to attend college and apply for driver's licenses and work permits without fear of deportation.

DACA granted these rights to around eight hundred thousand undocumented immigrants who were born after 1981, were brought to the United States before their sixteenth birthday, and have lived in the country since 2007. The largest concentrations of DACA recipients live in California (28 percent) and Texas (16 percent), with other large population residing in Illinois, New York, and Arizona. According to a 2017 survey conducted by the Center for American Progress, 69 percent of Dreamers were able to move to jobs with better pay after receiving DACA, and 8 percent started their own businesses. As one unnamed survey participant explains,

> Because of DACA, I opened a restaurant. We are contributing to the economic growth of our local community. We pay our fair share of taxes and hire employees. . . . I depend on my [DACA status] for a lot of my business, such as when getting licenses, permits, leases, and credit.[36]

Despite the positive aspects of the program, DACA has many critics. The biggest criticism involves how the program was created: President Obama bypassed Congress by issuing an executive order. For this and other reasons, Trump tried to end DACA. It has also been challenged in court but so far remains in effect. In 2019 House Democrats proposed legislation that would provide Dreamers with a path to citizenship. The Dream and Promise Act of 2019 would allow Dreamers to apply for ten-year green cards, which would be made permanent if they completed at least two years of college or military service or were employed for three years. However, political observers did not give the Dream and Promise Act a strong chance of ever becoming law.

A Divided Public

Americans remain divided over the status of Dreamers. Many support the view stated by Kris Kobach, Kansas's secretary of state, in 2017: "I would suggest [to DACA recipients]: Go home and get in line, come into the United States legally . . . then become a citizen."[37] In fact, there is no line a foreign-born person can get into to become a citizen. The citizenship process is long, complicated, and expensive. And the government requires most foreigners pursuing a legal pathway into the country to have special skills or relatives in the United States who are citizens. Because of various restrictions on people from Mexico, the citizenship process for an unmarried Mexican, twenty-one years old or older, could drag on for twenty-one years, according to the US Department of State.

> "I would suggest [to DACA recipients]: Go home and get in line, come into the United States legally . . . then become a citizen."[37]
>
> —Kris Kobach, Kansas's secretary of state

The only chance for Dreamers to obtain permanent legal status in the United States is for Congress to pass a law that provides them with a path to citizenship. According to a 2018 National Public Radio (NPR) poll, a majority of Americans support

The Stewart Detention Center

Being in the United States illegally is a misdemeanor, which is considered a minor offense akin to shoplifting or trespassing. Americans arrested for misdemeanors rarely face jail time. However, when ICE arrests undocumented immigrants, they are sent to ICE detention centers. Most of these prisons are located in rural areas, making it difficult for detainees to meet with relatives, immigrant advocates, and immigration lawyers. For example, the Stewart Detention Center is in the small village of Lumpkin, located 30 miles (48 km) south of Columbus, Georgia. The isolated town has one immigration lawyer for Stewart's eighteen hundred detainees and no hotels for visitors.

The Stewart Detention Center is run by the private prison corporation CoreCivic. The facility has numerous open dormitories, each one holding sixty-six prisoners in rows of bunk beds. Each dormitory has one bathroom with several sinks, toilets, and showers that often lack hot water. Residents are required to purchase toilet paper, soap, lotion, and toothpaste, along with phone cards that allow them to contact family members and lawyers.

One of the only ways for prisoners to get money to buy necessities is by participating in what the prison corporations call a voluntary work program. Detainees are paid one to four dollars a day to scrub toilets and floors, clean the medical center, cook meals, and wash prison laundry. Those who refuse to work or who protest prison conditions can be placed in solitary confinement for an extended period. In August 2018 CoreCivic was sued by three detainees over conditions at the detention center.

such legislation. The poll found that 65 percent of Americans say people brought to the United States as children, and who are now residing in the country illegally, should be granted legal status. As educator Mildred Garcia writes,

[Dreamers] have grown up and attended school in America as the only home many of them have known. . . . We have a moral obligation to enable them to continue to pursue the American Dream. That moral obligation happens to coincide with our national self-interest: These are young people who love this country and are hopeful to contribute to it as eagerly as anyone else.[38]

The NPR poll also shows that 67 percent of Americans believe that *all* undocumented immigrants, including adults, should be allowed to stay in the United States and eventually apply for citizenship. Support for that view has increased since 2016, when only 60 percent said they favored a path to citizenship for all undocumented immigrants.

Yet divisions remain. A Monmouth University poll conducted in early 2018 notes that most Americans see illegal immigration as a serious problem. In that poll, 45 percent said they considered illegal immigration to be a very serious problem, and another 25 percent identified it as somewhat serious. One often-expressed concern is that people who are here illegally should not be given priority over people who have followed the rules and waited, in some cases, for years for permission to immigrate legally. As long as the public remains divided, the future of undocumented people in the United States will be marked by uncertainty and fear.

CHAPTER FOUR

Seeking Solutions

S omething happened in Washington, DC, in 2013 that might seem nearly impossible today. A bipartisan group of senators—four Republicans and four Democrats—wrote a bill that provided comprehensive solutions to many of the problems that still exist in connection with illegal immigration. The Border Security, Economic Opportunity, and Immigration Modernization Act (also known as S.774) passed the full Senate, with sixty-eight votes in favor and thirty-two against.

The act provided a thirteen-year pathway that undocumented immigrants could follow to become citizens. Those who passed a background check, committed no major crimes, and paid a fee would achieve registered provisional immigrant (RPI) status. After thirteen years of working, paying taxes, and having no criminal record, those with RPI status could become citizens. One provision of the RPI program was the DREAM Act. The act included an accelerated five-year program that would provide RPI status to undocumented young people brought to the United States as children. As Phillip E. Wolgin, the director of immigration policy for the Center for American Progress, explains, "Once they gained RPI status, immigrants would be free from the constant worry that they or their family members could be picked up by police, detained, and deported at any time; they also would have the ability to work legally."[39]

Another part of S.744, the Comprehensive Southern Border Security Strategy, set aside a record-setting $46 billion for improving security measures along the US-Mexico border. The bill provided funds to double the number of Border Patrol officers from nineteen thousand to thirty-eight thousand and to construct 700 miles (1,126 km) of double- and triple-layer fencing along the border. In addition, a high-tech surveillance system with drones, cameras, and other technology would be deployed.

The nonpartisan Congressional Budget Office, which analyzes budget and economic information for Congress, said at the time that S.744 would save the United States $197 billion in border enforcement over ten years. And by providing legal status to undocumented workers, an estimated 145,000 jobs would be created, adding $1.2 trillion to the economy within a decade. As Wolgin explains, "Put simply, millions of people would be on their way to permanent legal status and citizenship, thousands of families across the nation would be together, and the U.S. economy would see significant gains."[40]

Senators who supported the bill were hopeful of passage in the House of Representatives, but that did not happen. The House refused to even consider the bill—or any others aimed at immigration reform. Conservative representatives in Congress argued that undocumented immigrants, who broke the law when they entered the United States, should be expelled—not granted citizenship. Without approval in the House, the Border Security, Economic Opportunity, and Immigration Modernization Act was dead.

Fix the Visa Overstay Problem

Although S.744 failed, experts on immigration and lawmakers from both political parties continue to advocate for immigration reforms similar to those in the 2013 Senate bill. Nonetheless, solutions remain elusive because partisan politics dominate the debate: when one side claims victory, the other side is seen as weak and defeated. However, there are policies that both sides seem to agree on and trade-offs partisans might consider. For example, most Democrats and Republicans agree that policies should be enacted that would prevent people from overstaying their visas.

Congress addressed the issue of overstays in 2002 by requiring an entry/exit tracking system at every border checkpoint. By 2007 the DHS had implemented a world-class entry system based on unique body characteristics called biometric identifiers. Foreign visa holders are required to provide border agents with fingerprints, face and eye scans, or other identifiers. However, exit tracking systems were not put into place to ensure that every visa holder left the country.

That changed in 2017 when the DHS instituted a $1 billion biometric exit program. The department installed facial recognition systems at outbound airline gates at some of the country's busiest airports, including those in Boston, Atlanta, Chicago, New York City, and Washington, DC. Foreign travelers on certain international outbound flights are required to stop before a sophisticated camera that transmits the traveler's photo to a database that confirms the face matches the traveler's entrance photo.

Using facial recognition software, a US Customs and Border Protection agent screens a family at Orlando International Airport in Florida in 2018. Biometric screening helps the federal government keep track of people who overstay their visas.

Experts have also suggested a less high-tech method to reduce visa overstays. Congress could require the DHS to use texts and email alerts to remind foreign travelers of their visa expiration dates while thanking them for on-time departures. Lawmakers could also fully fund programs that would prioritize overstay enforcement. According to C. Stewart Verdery Jr., former assistant secretary of the DHS, overstay enforcement has not been a priority. In 2017 ICE spent less than 10 percent of its enforcement budget on locating and deporting overstays. According to Verdery,

> A new initiative to identify, warn and if necessary remove recent visa overstays should be fully funded and implemented. As we have seen in the bitter fight over immigration reform, every day, week or month that a foreign visitor remains in the U.S. creates additional ties to the country—employment, family, community connections—that make a departure more disruptive to our families and businesses.[41]

Workplace Screening

As Verdery points out, many of those who enter the United States illegally are seeking employment. Those who support immigration reform agree that fewer would enter the country illegally if employers did more to screen out undocumented workers. This can be done using a DHS employment verification program called E-Verify. The Internet-based program cross-checks official government records with information like birth dates and Social Security numbers that employees enter on job application forms. If the information does not match, employers are alerted and the worker must resolve the problem or face dismissal.

Federal contractors have been required to use E-Verify since 2007. It has been voluntary for other businesses. According to the latest government figures, almost 750,000 US employers are enrolled in the program. Many immigration experts want Trump to make E-Verify mandatory for all employers. As former immigration judge Andrew R. Arthur explains, "There are many changes that could be made to the immigration laws that would enable the United States to gain control over its illegal population. Of all of the proposals, however, E-Verify would be the most effective at curbing illegal entries and limiting nonimmigrant overstays."[42]

As with every other issue that is tied to illegal immigration, there is disagreement on whether to make E-Verify mandatory. Groups as diverse as the progressive American Civil Liberties Union and the libertarian Cato Institute oppose E-Verify. They view the system as a government intrusion into the daily business affairs of average citizens. Critics also point out that the system is flawed. According to a Cato study, between 2006 and 2016 about 130,000 people lost their jobs due to E-Verify errors. When citizens and legal residents are misidentified as being undocumented, they have to spend untold amounts of time and money to correct errors over which they have no control.

> "E-Verify would be the most effective at curbing illegal entries and limiting nonimmigrant overstays."[42]
>
> —Andrew R. Arthur, a former immigration judge

While the number of errors seems large, supporters of E-Verify point out that millions of people are properly identified by the system every year. And E-Verify has been promoted by Democratic politicians; in 2011 Obama stated his desire to make E-Verify mandatory for companies that employ more than fifty people.

Reforming the Asylum System

Whether or not the E-Verify system is expanded, there still remains the more immediate problem of thousands of Central American families and individuals waiting at the border to present their cases for asylum. The immigration courts have an enor-

Solutions from the Sanctuary Movement

The Church World Service (CWS) is a leader in the sanctuary movement, which consists of more than one thousand interfaith congregations that offer safe havens for undocumented immigrants facing deportation. In 2018 the CWS published a list of policy recommendations meant to create a more just and humane immigration system. An excerpt appears below:

> The U.S. government should take every step to uphold family unity, respect and dignity to all immigrants regardless of their documentation status. . . .
>
> The [president's] administration should take into account risk factors of extremely dangerous countries at war or with high homicide rates and stop deporting people back to what could mean certain [death] . . . which is in keeping with our moral and legal obligations to offer protection.
>
> The administration should honor the profound violence faced by asylum seekers, unaccompanied children, refugees, and other vulnerable populations and see that they are welcomed and protected from being returned to harm or life-threatening conditions.
>
> Congress should immediately pass a permanent, legislative solution to offer a pathway to citizenship for as many dreamers as possible, like the Dream Act, without compromising family unity, border communities, or any other immigrant population.
>
> The administration, Congress, and all communities should strive toward creating long term policy solutions through legislation that lift up the core values of every faith tradition—to love ones neighbor and protect the inherent dignity and rights of every human being, including migrants, immigrants, and refugees.

Myrna Orozco and Noel Andersen, "Sanctuary in the Age of Trump," Church World Service, January 2018. www.sanctuarynotdeportation.org.

mous backlog of unresolved cases—and more cases are being added every day. Many asylum seekers are held under detention or supervised release as their claims make their way through the courts—a process that can take several years.

Immigration advocates are calling for the government to handle Central American asylum seekers the same way the Obama administration previously treated refugees from war-torn countries. During the Obama era, asylum applications from more than eighty thousand refugees from Syria, Iraq, and Afghanistan were processed annually. Rather than funnel their cases through immigration courts, these people were enrolled in the Refugee Resettlement Program (RRP) run by the Office of Refugee Resettlement.

In 2017 the number of refugees allowed into the country from Syria and Iraq was reduced by more than 98 percent by the Trump administration. A year later the United States resettled fewer than twenty-two thousand refugees, the lowest number in forty years. This left the RRP underutilized. Immigration rights supporters say that the resources of the RRP could be used to process one hundred thousand Central Americans asylum seekers per year.

A volunteer (left) assists a recent immigrant with her job search. Nonprofit organizations have demonstrated the ability to provide valuable resettlement help to new immigrants.

The RRP provides jobs and education through nonprofit, faith-based resettlement agencies like Catholic Charities, Lutheran Social Services, and the Hebrew Immigrant Aid Society. These agencies employ case managers, teachers, and supportive staff to work with asylum seekers and monitor each family. Refugees can see psychologists who specialize in treating people who have witnessed violence and suffered the types of trauma experienced by many refugees from the Northern Triangle.

Admitting Central American immigrants through the RRP would save the government millions of dollars. In 2018 the United States was spending about $8 million a day to detain all the people seeking asylum, around $208 per detainee. If the cases were handled by faith-based resettlement agencies, the cost would be around $5 per day per person. But diverting thousands of Central American asylum seekers to the RRP is about more than saving money, as Jodi Ziesemer, an attorney for Catholic Charities Community Services, explains:

> This would mean the end of the zero-tolerance policy of criminally prosecuting migrants. In its place, Refugee Resettlement would use existing programming to help migrants find housing, learn English, enroll children in schools, and respect American values and freedoms. These programs . . . are located in cities and rural areas, effectively dispersing a large number of refugees to areas that need labor and can support new settlers.[43]

The faith-based agencies that work with the RRP have a record of success going back decades. Those who pass through the RRP find jobs quickly. And numerous studies show that the refugees are doing more than supporting themselves. The resettlement costs refugees incur are paid back many times over through income taxes they pay over the course of their work lives. As Ziesemer explains, "The choice is not, as President Trump declared, between detaining families and quickly deporting them, or paroling them with no accountability. Using the resources and programs we have developed over the past century to help refugees, we can welcome asylum seekers humanely."[44]

Protecting Agricultural Workers

Many Central American asylum seekers are experienced agricultural workers. And US farmers depend on undocumented workers since most Americans are unwilling to perform the difficult work of planting fields, tending crops, and harvesting and packing produce. In California, which employs more agricultural workers than any other state, farmers in 2018 were faced with a severe labor shortage after ICE conducted a series of raids on farms. Some of those arrested had been in the country for decades, prompting undocumented Mexican worker Melitón Ferred to say, "Who is going to work the fields? No one. This is a difficult job, and all of us are from Mexico."[45]

"Using the resources and programs we have developed over the past century to help refugees, we can welcome asylum seekers humanely."[44]

—Jodi Ziesemer, attorney

The ICE raids spread fear though California's Central Valley, where many farms are located. But two California Democrats, Senator Dianne Feinstein and Representative Zoe Lofgren, believe they have a solution to the labor problem. The Agricultural Worker Program Act of 2019 would allow undocumented workers with two years of farmwork experience to apply for a permit—a blue card—which would allow them to legally work in agriculture in any state. The program would provide incentives for workers to maintain their blue card status. After five years of work, they would be able to apply for a green card that would grant them permanent lawful residence in the United States.

Feinstein says that California farmworkers have contributed significantly to the state's economy, even as they have become a priority for deportation by the Trump administration. According to Feinstein, the Agricultural Worker Program Act would be a win for everyone:

> Farmers throughout California struggle mightily to find workers, and we all know that backbreaking farm labor is performed largely by undocumented immigrants. By protecting farmworkers from deportation, our bill would ensure that hardworking immigrants don't live in fear and that California's agriculture industry has the workforce it needs to succeed. . . . We must protect the families who help put food on our tables.[46]

The Agricultural Worker Program Act of 2019 was supported by Western Growers, an agriculture trade group that usually aligns itself with conservative politicians. And a dozen senators and sixty-one House members hoped to advance the bill. However, many senators viewed the program as a way to grant amnesty for undocumented workers. In the political climate of the day, the fate of the bill was in doubt.

Immigration Trade-Offs

DACA recipients are another group whose lives are overshadowed by unpredictable political realities. In January 2018 the Trump administration issued a framework for Congress that would permanently protect Dreamers. The framework would open a ten- to twelve-year pathway to citizenship for seven hundred thousand DACA holders in exchange for limiting what Trump calls chain migration. Trump and others use this term in place of what is officially called family reunification or family-based immigration by the USCIS.

Family reunification is a process used by foreign-born immigrants who have legally become US citizens. These people can sponsor immediate family members who wish to immigrate to the

In January 2018 President Donald Trump issued a framework for a proposed immigration bill. The White House would protect undocumented young people (Dreamers) in exchange for tough security measures, including construction of a massive border wall. The Trump framework asserts that

> securing the . . . border of the United States takes a combination of physical infrastructure, technology, personnel, resources, authorities, and the ability to close legal loopholes that are exploited by smugglers, traffickers, cartels, criminals and terrorists.
>
> The Department of Homeland Security must have the tools to deter illegal immigration. . . . These measures below are the minimum tools necessary to mitigate the rapidly growing surge of illegal immigration.
>
> - $25 billion trust fund for the border wall system, ports of entry/exit, and northern border improvements and enhancements.
> - Close crippling personnel deficiencies by appropriating additional funds to hire new DHS personnel, ICE attorneys, immigration judges, prosecutors and other law enforcement professionals. . . .
> - Deter illegal entry . . . by closing legal loopholes that have eroded our ability to secure the immigration system and protect public safety.
> - Ensure the detention and removal of criminal aliens, gang members, violent offenders, and aggravated felons.
> - Ensure the prompt removal of illegal border-crossers regardless of country of origin.
> - Deter visa overstays with efficient removal. . . .
> - Provide legal status for DACA recipients and other DACA-eligible illegal immigrants . . . [by implementing a] 10–12 year path to citizenship, with requirements for work, education and good moral character.

White House, "White House Framework on Immigration Reform & Border Security," January 25, 2018. www.whitehouse.gov.

United States. Relatives who are eligible for family reunification include spouses, children, and parents of adult children. Other relatives—including aunts, uncles, cousins, and grandparents—cannot obtain visas under the family reunification process. Qualifying relatives who obtain green cards are allowed to work and permanently live in the United States.

The family reunification process is the most commonly used type of legal immigration to the United States. In 2016 nearly 567,000 foreign-born immediate relatives of US citizens obtained permanent visas through the program. This figure represents around 65 percent of all lawful permanent immigration to the United States. Trump and others who wish to limit legal immigration want to change the program so that only spouses and unmarried minor children qualify for family reunification. They believe that this change would help limit the number of immigrants and clear a backlog of more than 3.7 million immigrants waiting in line for green cards.

Trump's proposal to offer a path to citizenship for Dreamers while limiting family reunification was viewed as a solution to the DACA problem by some of his supporters. Steven Camarota is the director of research for the Center for Immigration Studies, a Washington, DC, think tank that supports drastically reducing the number of immigrants legally allowed into the United States. Camarota has opposed measures to legalize Dreamers, but he believes DACA recipients are never going to be deported due to public support for their cause. Camarota says he could support providing a path to citizenship for Dreamers in exchange for reducing the number qualifying for family reunification: "Eventually, [DACA recipients are] going to become Americans, and you want them to fully participate in your society."[47]

"Eventually, [DACA recipients are] going to become Americans, and you want them to fully participate in your society."[47]

—Steven Camarota, the director of research for the Center for Immigration Studies

Seeking Change Through Political Activism

Camarota's comment shows that some anti-immigration hard-liners are willing to compromise. But many Dreamers believe the best way to solve their political problem is to encourage voters to elect politicians who are sympathetic to their dilemma. Gabriela Cruz is one of those Dreamers. She was brought to California illegally by her grandmother in 1990, when she was only one year old. Cruz was unaware of her undocumented status until she was in eighth grade. At that time, her grandmother explained that Cruz's undocumented status would prevent her from attending college, getting a driver's license, or applying for a job.

Cruz's life changed dramatically in 2011. California passed a state law called the California Dream Act, which began providing financial aid and in-state tuition for students without legal status. In 2012 Obama implemented the federal DACA program, which provided additional protection to Cruz and thousands of other young immigrants. With her DACA status secured, Cruz went to college and got a good job. But when Trump attempted to rescind DACA in 2017, she quit her job and became a political activist. Cruz joined an immigrant rights organization founded by DACA recipients called United We Dream. She founded a local United We Dream chapter in her hometown of Santa Cruz, California, and since then has been actively working for the election of congressional candidates who she believes will help Dreamers achieve their goal of full US citizenship.

A Political Disagreement

While experts on both sides of the political divide consider ways to solve immigration problems, most Americans have already made up their minds. Polls consistently show that around two-thirds of Americans want to allow Dreamers to remain in the United States if they meet certain requirements, such as working or going to school. According to a 2018 Gallup poll, around 60

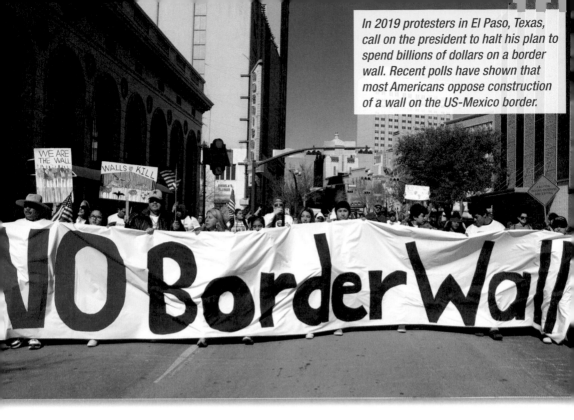

In 2019 protesters in El Paso, Texas, call on the president to halt his plan to spend billions of dollars on a border wall. Recent polls have shown that most Americans oppose construction of a wall on the US-Mexico border.

percent of Americans opposed building a wall across the US-Mexico border, and 65 percent said Congress should work to provide a pathway for all undocumented immigrants to lawfully reside in the United States.

With broad public support, solutions to illegal immigration issues should not be that difficult to implement. As Tom Jawetz, the vice president of the Center for American Progress, says, "I don't think this is a major policy disagreement or a terribly difficult policy to enact. It's a political disagreement at its heart."[48]

It is often said that politics is the art of compromise, but many politicians refuse to cooperate and negotiate with opposing factions. This inflexibility has left the millions of undocumented immigrants in limbo and has had a very real effect on people's lives. As Cruz states, "We shouldn't be living in a world of fear because we are undocumented."[49]

> "We shouldn't be living in a world of fear because we are undocumented."[49]
>
> —Gabriela Cruz, Dreamer activist

SOURCE NOTES

Introduction: What Sort of Crisis Is This?

1. Quoted in Dana Farrington, "Transcript: Trump's Address on Border Security and Democratic Response," NPR, January 8, 2019. www.npr.org.
2. Quoted in Farrington, "Transcript."
3. Quoted in Patrick J. McDonnell, "First in Migrant Caravan Reach Mexico City, Still Hundreds of Miles from U.S. Border," *Los Angeles Times*, November 5, 2018. www.latimes.com.
4. Quoted in *Time* Staff, "Here's Donald Trump's Presidential Announcement Speech," *Time*, June 16, 2015. http://time.com.
5. Quoted in CNN, "Read: Trump's Memo Ordering National Guard Troops to the Border," April 4, 2018. www.cnn.com.
6. Quoted in Jordan Fabian, "Trump: Migrant Caravan 'Is an Invasion,'" *The Hill* (Washington, DC), October 29, 2018. https://thehill.com.
7. Michael H. Fuchs, "Forget the 'Border Crisis'—It Is Trump's Shutdown That Makes Us Less Safe," *Guardian* (Manchester, UK), January 20, 2019. www.theguardian.com.

Chapter One: The Caravan from Central America

8. Quoted in Kevin Sieff and Josh Partlow, "How the Migrant Caravan Became So Big and Why It's Continuing to Grow," MSN, October 24, 2018. www.msn.com.
9. Quoted in Andrea Domínguez, "Donald Trump Cuts Aid to Honduras and Guatemala, but Migrants Continue to the US," GuateVision, October 22, 2018. www.guatevision.com.
10. Quoted in Sieff and Partlow, "How the Migrant Caravan Became So Big and Why It's Continuing to Grow."

11. Quoted in Jonathan Blitzer, "On the Desperate and Uncertain Trail of the Migrant Caravan," *New Yorker*, October 26, 2018. www.newyorker.com.

12. Quoted in Delphine Schrank, "A Day in the Life of a Family in the Migrant Caravan," ABC News, November 4, 2018. https://abcnews.go.com.

13. Quoted in UN News, "2,300 Migrant Children in Central American 'Caravan' Need Protection, UNICEF Says," October 26, 2018. https://news.un.org.

14. US Citizenship and Immigration Services, "Refugees & Asylum," November 2015. www.uscis.gov.

15. León Krauze, "'God Willing, We Can Cross and My Dream Will Come True,'" *Slate*, November 30, 2018. https://slate.com.

16. Quoted in Ben Ashford, "Hundreds of Migrants Begin to 'Self-Deport,'" *Daily Mail* (London), November 29, 2018. www.dailymail.co.uk.

17. Blitzer, "On the Desperate and Uncertain Trail of the Migrant Caravan."

18. Quoted in Sarah Kinosian and Joshua Partlow, "U.S. Closes Major Crossing as Caravan Migrants Mass at Border in Mexico," *Washington Post*, November 26, 2018. www.washingtonpost.com.

19. Quoted in Kinosian and Partlow, "U.S. Closes Major Crossing as Caravan Migrants Mass at Border in Mexico."

20. Quoted in Gustavo Solis, "Migrants Tell U.S.: Let Us in or Pay Us," *Los Angeles Times*, December 13, 2018, p. A4.

Chapter Two: Refugees in Search of a Safe Haven

21. Jennifer Vannette, "How Human Rights Gained International Support," *Washington Post*, December 17, 2018. www.washingtonpost.com.

22. United Nations, "Universal Declaration of Human Rights," 2018. www.un.org.

23. Quoted in Mica Rosenberg, Reade Levinson, and Ryan McMeill, "They Fled Danger at Home to Make a High-Stakes Bet on U.S. Immigration Courts," Reuters, October 17, 2017. www.reuters.com.

24. Quoted in Phillip Bump, "Here Are the Administration Officials Who Have Said That Family Separation Is Meant as a Deterrent," *Washington Post*, June 19, 2018. www.washingtonpost.com.

25. Dan Berry et al., "Cleaning Toilets, Following Rules: A Migrant Child's Day in Detention," *New York Times*, June 14, 2018. www.nytimes.com.

26. Quoted in Stephen Collinson and Lauren Fox, "Outrage Grows as Families Are Separated. Will Trump Change His Policy?," CNN, June 18, 2018. www.cnn.com.

27. Quoted in *New York Times*, "Kirstjen Nielsen Addresses Family Separation at Border: Full Transcript," June 18, 2018. www.nytimes.com.

28. Quoted in Ginger Thomas, "Families Are Still Being Separated at the Border, Months After 'Zero Tolerance' Was Reversed," ProPublica, November 27, 2018. www.propublica.org.

29. Miriam Jordan, "Ninth Circuit Appeals Court Grants More Protections for Asylum Seekers," *New York Times*, March 7, 2019. www.nytimes.com

Chapter Three: The Undocumented Immigrants

30. Quoted in BBC News, "Migrant Caravan: What Is It and Why Does It Matter?," November 26, 2018. www.bbc.com.

31. Quoted in Stuart Anderson, "There Is No Crisis at the Border—and DHS Stats Prove It," *Forbes*, June 25, 2017. www.forbes.com.

32. Quoted in David M. Reimers, *Still the Golden Door: The Third World Comes to America*. New York: Columbia University Press, 1992, p. 220.

33. Quoted in NPR Staff, "A Reagan Legacy: Amnesty for Illegal Immigrants," NPR, July 4, 2010. www.npr.org.

34. Quoted in Shelli King, "The Current Border Debate Has Me Confused," Quora, June 20, 2018. www.quora.com.

35. Quoted in Maris Franco and Carlos Garcia, "The Deportation Machine Obama Built for President Trump," *Nation*, June 27, 2016. www.thenation.com.

36. Quoted in Tom K. Wong et al., "DACA Recipients' Economic and Educational Gains Continue to Grow," Center for American Progress, August 28, 2017. www.americanprogress.org.

37. Quoted in Priscilla Alvarez, "What the Waiting List for Legal Residency Actually Looks Like," *Atlantic*, September 17, 2017. www.theatlantic.com.

38. Mildred Garcia, "Fix DACA and Move On," *U.S. News & World Report*, January 19, 2018. www.usnews.com.

Chapter Four: Seeking Solutions

39. Phillip E. Wolgin, "2 Years Later, Immigrants Are Still Waiting on Immigration Reform," Center for American Progress, June 24, 2015. www.americanprogress.org.

40. Wolgin, "2 Years Later, Immigrants Are Still Waiting on Immigration Reform."

41. C. Stewart Verdery Jr., "Solving Visa Overstays: How Technology Can Lead to Reform," *The Hill* (Washington, DC), September 15, 2017. https://thehill.com.

42. Quoted in Paul Bedard, "Trump Urged to Nationalize 'E-Verify' After 700 Percent Surge in Arrests of Illegal Workers," *Washington Examiner*, December 28, 2018. www.washingtonexaminer.com.

43. Jodi Ziesemer, "A Solution to the US Border Crisis? Treat Detained Migrants as Refugees," *Guardian* (Manchester, UK), August 5, 2018. www.theguardian.com.

44. Ziesemer, "A Solution to the US Border Crisis?"

45. Quoted in Andrea Castillo, "ICE Arrests Farmworkers, Spreading Fears in the Central Valley over Immigrants and the Economy," *Los Angeles Times*, March 31, 2018. www.latimes.com.

46. Quoted in Jessica Donnel, "Agriculture Worker Program Act of 2019 Proposes New Paths to Legal Employment and Citizenship," And Now UKnow, January 18, 2019. www.and nowuknow.com.

47. Quoted in Julia Preston, "We Locked Four Experts in a Room Until They Solved Immigration," Politico, February 9, 2018. www.politico.com.

48. Quoted in Preston, "We Locked Four Experts in a Room Until They Solved Immigration."

49. Quoted in Jazmine Ulloa, "How Young Immigrant 'Dreamers' Made Flipping Control of the House a Personal Quest," *Los Angeles Times*, January 1, 2019. www.latimes.com.

ORGANIZATIONS AND WEBSITES

American Civil Liberties Union (ACLU)
125 Broad St., 18th Floor
New York, NY 10004
website: www.aclu.org

The ACLU works in the courts, legislatures, and communities to preserve and defend the individual rights and liberties that the US Constitution guarantees to everyone in the country. The ACLU's Immigrants' Rights Project addresses immigration issues that include workplace rights, detention and deportation, and discrimination.

Center for Immigration Studies (CIS)
1629 K St. NW, Suite 600
Washington, DC 20006
website: www.cis.org

The CIS is an independent, nonprofit research organization that publishes a variety of reports and articles that examine the social, economic, environmental, security, and economic consequences of both legal and illegal immigration. The CIS believes that debates informed by objective data will lead to better immigration policies.

Federation for American Immigration Reform (FAIR)
25 Massachusetts Ave. NW, Suite 330
Washington, DC 20001
website: www.fairus.org

FAIR is a national nonprofit organization of citizens who share the belief that America's immigration policies must be reformed to serve the national interest. FAIR seeks to stop all illegal immigration, favors greatly enhanced border security, and supports policies that would lower legal immigration levels.

Heritage Foundation
214 Massachusetts Ave. NE
Washington, DC 20002-4999
website: www.heritage.org

Founded in 1973, the Heritage Foundation is a research and educational institution that seeks to formulate and promote conservative public policies. It supports immigration policies that protect immigrants who enter the United States through legal channels and advocates sharp measures to deter illegal immigration.

Migration Policy Institute
1400 Sixteenth St. NW, Suite 300
Washington, DC 20036
website: www.migrationpolicy.org

This nonpartisan institute conducts authoritative research and publishes the online journal *Migration Information Source* with the goal of improving immigration policy through learning and dialogue. The institute has offices in the United States and Europe to provide a global perspective to immigration issues.

National Immigration Forum
50 F St. NW, Suite 300
Washington, DC 20001
website: www.immigrationforum.org

The National Immigration Forum advocates for the rights of all immigrants and promotes federal immigration policies that embrace America's tradition as a nation of immigrants. The forum publishes and distributes a wide range of educational materials, including fact sheets, issue papers, and other reading materials.

US Citizenship and Immigration Services (USCIS)

Department of Homeland Security
Washington, DC 20528
website: www.uscis.gov

A branch of the US Department of Homeland Security, the USCIS oversees lawful immigration into the United States. This includes granting all immigration and citizenship benefits and setting policies regarding who will be allowed to enter the United States. Its website provides information on current immigration laws and regulations.

FOR FURTHER RESEARCH

Books

Stephen Currie, *Undocumented Immigrant Youth*. San Diego: ReferencePoint, 2017.

Jim Gallagher, *Thinking Critically: Illegal Immigration*. San Diego: ReferencePoint, 2019.

Diane Guerrero and Erica Moroz, *My Family Divided: One Girl's Journey of Home, Loss, and Hope*. New York: Square Fish, 2019.

Susan Kuklin, *We Are Here to Stay: Voices of Undocumented Young Adults*. New York: Candlewick, 2019.

Stephanie Sammartino McPherson, *The Global Refugee Crisis: Fleeing Conflict and Violence*. Minneapolis: Twenty-First Century, 2019.

Erin Staley, *I'm an Undocumented Immigrant. Now What?* New York: Rosen Young Adult, 2017.

Internet Sources

Abby Castro, "La Bestia and the Struggle of Central American Migrants," ERSI, 2016. www.arcgis.com.

Hillary Goodfriend, "The Honduran Nightmare," *Jacobin*, December 12, 2018. www.jacobinmag.com.

Myrna Orozco and Noel Andersen, "Sanctuary in the Age of Trump," Church World Service, January 2018. www.sanctuary notdeportation.org.

Julia Preston, "We Locked Four Experts in a Room Until They Solved Immigration," Politico, February 9, 2018. www.politico .com.

United Nations, "Universal Declaration of Human Rights," 2018. www.un.org.

Websites

American Friends Service Committee (www.afsc.org). The committee was founded in 1917 to promote peace and justice. It provides immigrants with information about sanctuary, financial aid, employment, and education.

NumbersUSA (www.numbersusa.com). NumbersUSA says it is a pro-immigrant organization that seeks to reduce immigration to the United States by limiting family reunification and other government programs.

ReliefWeb (https://reliefweb.int). ReliefWeb is a digital service of the UN Office for the Coordination of Humanitarian Affairs. The website provides key information, including reports, maps, and infographics about global immigration crises and disasters.

United We Dream (https://unitedwedream.org). United We Dream was founded by DACA recipients to promote the interests of Dreamers brought to the United States illegally as children. Its website provides critical data about political campaigns, border security issues, and changes in immigration law.

WOLA (www.wola.org). The Washington Office of Latin America, which goes by the name WOLA, advocates for human rights in the Americas with the goal of promoting justice and reducing violence. The organization's website features news, analysis, and a "get involved" section that promotes events, student internships, and various campaigns.

INDEX

Note: Boldface page numbers indicate illustrations.

immigration reform
framework issued by, 57,
58, 59
opposition to illegal
immigration as signature
issue of, 6–7
reduces number of refugees
from Syria/Iraq, 54

unaccompanied minors
children separated from
parents categorized as,
27
detention of, 27–28
underground economy, 38–39
United Nations (UN), 11
United Nations Children's Fund
(UNICEF), 11
Universal Declaration of
Human Rights (UDHR), 20,
33

US Citizenship and
Immigration Services
(USCIS), 13, 69
U.S. News & World Report,
36–37

Vannette, Jennifer, 20
Verdery, C. Stewart, Jr., 51
violence, in Northern Triangle,
11, 13
visa overstays, 36
solutions to, 49–51

Wagner, Steven, 27
Washington, John, 11
Western Growers, 57
Williams, Tracie, 11
Wolgin, Phillip E., 48, 49
workplace raids, 40, 41

Ziesemer, Jodi, 55–56

PICTURE CREDITS

ABOUT THE AUTHOR

Stuart A. Kallen is the author of more than 350 nonfiction books for children and young adults. He has written on topics ranging from the theory of relativity to the art of electronic dance music. In 2018 Kallen won a Green Earth award from the Nature Generation environmental organization for his book *Trashing the Planet: Examining the Global Garbage Glut*. In his spare time he is a singer, songwriter, and guitarist in San Diego.